UPDATED EDITION

Guess What!

Student's Book 2B
with eBook

American English

Susannah Reed with Kay Bentley

Series Editor: Lesley Koustaff

CAMBRIDGE

Contents

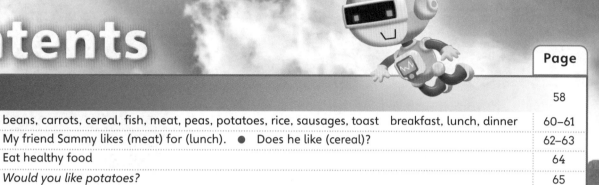

5 Meals

Look!

Guess What!

1 🎧 5.01 **Listen. Who's speaking?**

2 🎧 5.02 **Listen, point, and say.**

The Caf...
Breakfast 8—
Lunch 12—
Dinner 4—

1 potatoes
2 carrots
3 rice
4 peas
5 sausages
6 fish
7 meat
8 beans
9 toast
10 cereal

Find Leo

3 🎧 5.03 **Listen and find.**

4 Say the chant.

Do you like toast for breakfast?
Do you like cereal, too?
Toast and cereal for breakfast?
Yum! Yes, I do.

breakfast

lunch

dinner

5 Read, look, and say. What's missing?

Shopping list

cereal

sausages

meat

peas

potatoes

beans

rice

fish

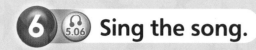

6 🎧 5.06 **Sing the song.**

My friend Sammy likes 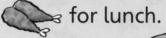 for lunch.
He doesn't like 🥔,
And he doesn't like 🫛.
He likes 🫘 and 🥕,
And he likes 🧀.

Munch, Sammy.
Munch your lunch!

My friend Sally likes 🐟 for lunch.
She doesn't like 🧀,
And she doesn't like 🍗.
She likes 🫘 and 🥕,
And 🥔 and 🫛.

Munch, Sally.
Munch your lunch!

7 🎧 5.07 **Listen and say *Sammy* or *Sally*.**

8 (About Me) **Ask and answer. Then say.**

Do you like fish?

Yes, I do.

Alex likes fish.

Grammar: *My friend Sammy likes meat for lunch.* → Workbook page 50

9 🎧 5.09 Listen, look, and say.

1

2

10 (Think) Ask and answer.

Tony

Kim

Is it a boy or a girl?

It's a boy.

Does he like meat?

Yes, he does.

Does he like carrots?

No, he doesn't.

It's Tony!

Tom

Pat

→ Workbook page 51

Grammar: *Does he like cereal?*

Grammar fun!

1. Look! Café Hawaii!

   Café Hawaii

   Let's go for lunch!

2. Café Hawaii

   Would you like fish and potatoes?

   Yes, please!

   No, thank you!

3. What about carrots or peas, iPal?

   No, thank you!

4. Oh, dear! What would you like, iPal?

   Cake! I like chocolate cake.

5. More cake, please!

   No, iPal. That's enough!

6. What's the matter?

   He likes chocolate cake – a lot!

→ Workbook page 52

12 5.12 (Talk Time) **Listen and act.**

Animal sounds

13 5.13 **Listen and say.**

A seal in the sun. A zebra in the zoo.

What kind of **food** is it?

1 🎧 5.15 **Listen and say.**

| fruit | vegetables | meat | grains | dairy |

2 CLIL ▶ **Watch the video.**

Guess What!

3 **Look and say what kind of food it is.**

Number 1. Fish.   Yes.

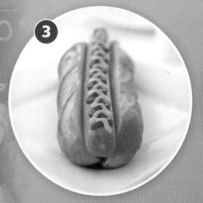

Let's collaborate!

OUR NEW HEALTHY CAFÉ MENU

lunch   discuss   dinner
breakfast   present
create

→ Workbook page 54   CLIL: Science   **67**

6 Activities

Look!

Guess What!

69

1 (6.01) **Listen. Who's speaking?**

2 (6.02) **Listen, point, and say.**

Activity Day What can you do?

1 play tennis 2 play field hockey 3 play basketball

4 roller-skate 5 play baseball

6 ride a horse 7 fly a kite 8 take photographs

TODAY!

Find Leo

3 (6.03) **Listen and find.**

4 🎧 6.04 Say the chant.

I can play tennis.
I can't play field hockey.
Let's play tennis.
Good idea!

basketball
baseball

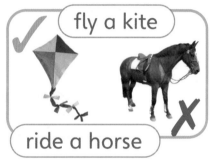
fly a kite
ride a horse

take photographs
roller-skate

5 (About Me) Match and say.

1, e. I can roller-skate.

1 I can roller-skate.
2 I can take photographs.
3 I can ride a horse.
4 I can play tennis.
5 I can play field hockey.

 a
 b
 c
 d
 e

6 (About Me) Point and tell your friend.

Picture b. I can play tennis.

Picture e. I can't roller-skate.

7 🎧 6.06 Listen, look, and say.

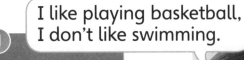

1 I like playing basketball, I don't like swimming.

2 I like swimming. I don't like playing basketball.

8 🎧 6.07 Listen and say the name.

Ann

Pam

Jack

Bill

Alex

Grace

9 About Me Things you like. Think and say.

I like painting.   He likes painting.

Grammar fun!

Grammar: *I like playing basketball.*   → Workbook page 58

10 🎧 6.08 Sing the song.

Do you like ?
No, I don't. No, I don't.
Do you like ?
Yes, I do. Yes, I do.
I like !

Does he like ?
No, he doesn't. No, he doesn't.
Does he like ?
Yes, he does. Yes, he does.
He likes !

Do you like ?
No, I don't. No, I don't.
Do you like ?
Yes, I do. Yes, I do.
I like !

Does she like ?
No, she doesn't. No, she doesn't.
Does she like ?
Yes, she does. Yes, she does.
She likes !

11 🎧 6.09 Think Listen and say the number.

1

2

3

4

5

6

Grammar: *Do you like flying a kite?*

74 Value: Play nicely

→ Workbook page 60

13 **Talk Time** **Listen and act.**

Animal sounds

14 6.13 **Listen and say.**

A camel with a camera. A kangaroo with a kite.

What equipment do we need?

1 🎧 6.15 Listen and say.

rackets   **sticks**   **bats**   **balls**

2 CLIL ▶ Watch the video.

3 Look and say *racket*, *stick*, *bat*, or *ball*.

Number 1. Ball.   Yes!

Guess What!

Let's collaborate!

actions   agree   present

LET'S **EXPLAIN A GAME**

body parts   team   find out

→ Workbook page 62   **CLIL: Sports**   **77**

Review Units 5 and 6

1 Look and say the words.

> Number 1. Fly a kite.

2 🎧 6.16 Listen and say the color.

Sue

Dan

→ Workbook pages 64–65

Look!

Guess What!

8

81

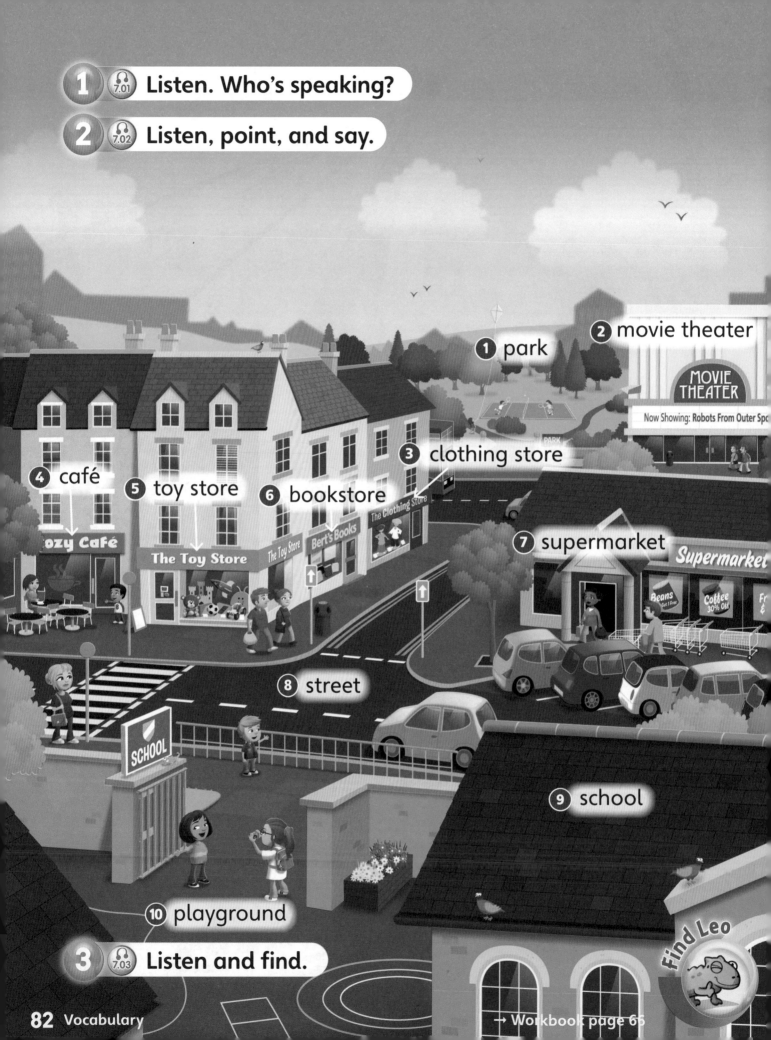

1 🎧 7.01 **Listen. Who's speaking?**

2 🎧 7.02 **Listen, point, and say.**

1 park

2 movie theater

3 clothing store

4 café

5 toy store

6 bookstore

7 supermarket

8 street

9 school

10 playground

3 🎧 7.03 **Listen and find.**

Find Leo

4 🎧 7.04 Say the chant.

Come with me and look around.
Who's in the café in the town?
It's my sister! She's in the café.
She's in the café in the town.

sister

brother

mom   dad

5 Match and say.

1, c. My cousin's on the playground.

a

b

1 My cousin's on the playground.
2 My aunt's in the clothing store.
3 My uncle's in the school.
4 My grandma's in the supermarket.
5 My grandpa's at the park.

c

d

e

6 Think Think of a place. Say and guess.

There's a desk and green chairs.

It's a school.

→ Workbook page 67

7 🎧 (7.06) **Sing the song.**

Come and visit my town,
My friendly little town.
It's nice to be in my town,
My little town.

There's a toy store and
a clothing store.
There's a bookstore
and a movie theater.
There's a café, and
there's a supermarket.
In my little town.

And the toy store is behind the
clothing store.
And the bookstore is in front of
the clothing store.
And the clothing store is between
the bookstore and the toy store!
In my little town.

And the movie theater is next to the café.
And the café is next to the supermarket.
And the café is between the supermarket
and the movie theater.

Come and visit my town …

8 🎧 (7.07) **Look, listen, and find the mistakes.**

The movie theater is next
to the supermarket.

No, it isn't. The movie theater
is next to the café.

Grammar: *The toy store is behind the clothing store.* → Workbook page 68

9 **7.08** **Listen, look, and say.**

Is there a playground behind the school?

Yes, there is.

Is there a café next to the movie theater?

No, there isn't.

10 **7.09** **Listen and say yes or no.**

11 **Think** **Play the game.**

Is there a café in front of the supermarket?

Yes, there is.

The movie theater is next to the school.

No, it isn't. The movie theater is next to the supermarket.

1. Movie tickets!
They're from my cousin, Anna!

2. Where's the movie theater?
It's next to the supermarket.

3. Let's go!
No, iPal! Be careful!

4. Look left and right.
It's safe now. Let's cross.

5. Oh, no! It's closed today!
NOW SHOWING
The Queen
Come with me!

6. It's a movie about robots!
I like going to the movies.

13   **Listen and act.**

Animal sounds

14 (7.13) **Listen and say.**

A quick queen bee. An ox with an X-ray.

→ Workbook page 71　　Functional language: *It's safe now. Let's cross.*　　Pronunciation: *qu, x*　**87**

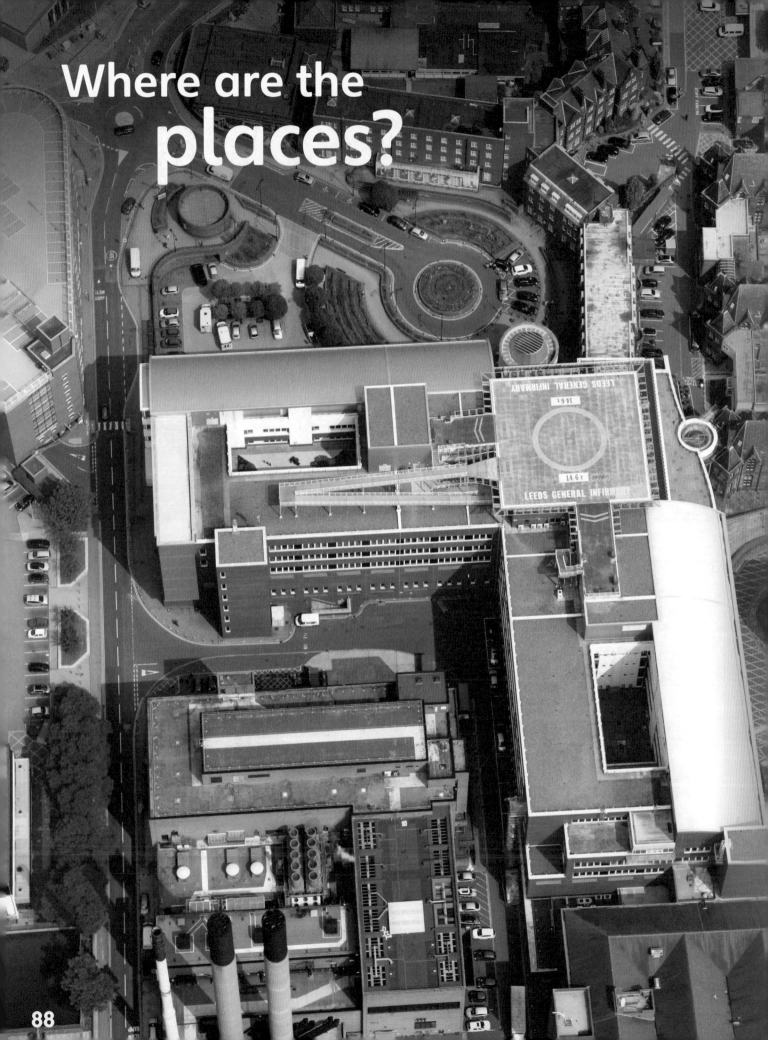

Where are the
places?

1 🎧 7.15 **Listen and say.**

police station

fire station

hospital

sports center

2 CLIL ▶ **Watch the video.**

3 **Look and say the letter and number.**

A, 3.   Fire station.   Yes!

Guess What!

Let's collaborate!

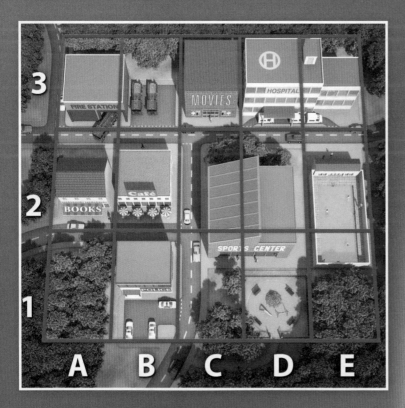

OUR IDEAL TOWN
make
draw
eco-friendly
bus stop
play
park

Look!

▶

Guess What!

theme

1 🎧 8.01 **Listen. Who's speaking?**

2 🎧 8.02 **Listen, point, and say.**

Café and Gift Store

1 field

2 barn

3 horse

4 donkey

5 sheep

6 goat

7 cow

8 duck

3 🎧 8.03 **Listen and find.**

9 pond

Find Leo

4 8.04 Say the chant.

donkey

Where's the donkey?
It's in the barn.
It's in the barn.
On the farm.

Where are the goats?
They're in the field.
They're in the field.
On the farm.

goats

cow

ducks

5 Read and follow. Then ask and answer.

Where's the cow?   It's in the field.

1  Where's the cow?

2 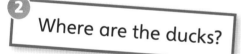 Where are the ducks?

3 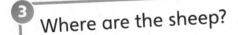 Where are the sheep?

4 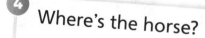 Where's the horse?

a

b

c

6 About Me Ask and answer.

What's your favorite animal?   It's a sheep.

7 🎧 8.06 Sing the song.

Field and pond, house and barn,
Look at the animals on the farm …

What's the 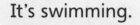 doing?
It's swimming. It's swimming.
It's swimming.
What's the doing?
It's swimming in the .

Field and pond …

What's the doing?
It's running. It's running. It's running.
What's the doing?
It's running in the .

Field and pond …

What's the doing?
It's sleeping. It's sleeping.
It's sleeping.
What's the doing?
It's sleeping in the .

Field and pond …

What's the doing?
It's eating. It's eating. It's eating.
What's the doing?
It's eating in the .

Field and pond …

8 🎧 8.07 Listen and answer the questions.

What's the duck doing?   It's swimming.

Grammar fun!

Grammar: *What's the duck doing?*   → Workbook page 76

9 🎧 8.08 **Listen, look, and say.**

1 Is the cat sleeping?   Yes, it is.

2 Is the duck swimming?   No, it isn't. It's flying.

10 Think **Play the game.**

Is the dog running?   Yes, it is.

Picture 1!

→ Workbook page 77   Grammar: *Is the cat sleeping?*   Grammar fun! ▶   **95**

It's a message for iPal.

Let's find him!

Would you like to come to a party?

Yes, please!

Hold on!

We're flying!

Welcome to the party!

It's so nice to see you!

WELCOME HOME i

What's Ben doing?

He's … dancing!

Goodbye, iPal!

Goodbye! Thanks for taking care of me!

96 Value: Love your home

→ Workbook page 78

12   **Listen and act.**

Animal sounds

13 **Listen and say.**

A wolf in the water. A white whale with a wheel.

Functional language: *Would you like to come to my party?*
Pronunciation: *w, wh*   **97**

What do
farmers do?

1 8.15 Listen and say.

plant seeds

turn soil

water plants

harvest plants

2 CLIL Watch the video.

3 Look and say.

Number 1. He turns soil.   Yes!

Guess What!

Let's collaborate!

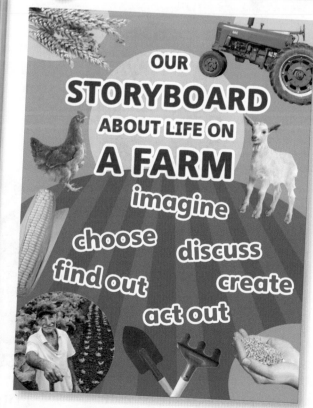

OUR STORYBOARD ABOUT LIFE ON A FARM

imagine

choose   discuss

find out   create

act out

Review Units 7 and 8

1 Look and say the words.

Number 1. Café.

2 🎧8.16 Listen and say the name.

Grace

Lola

Kento

Dan

3 Ask and answer.

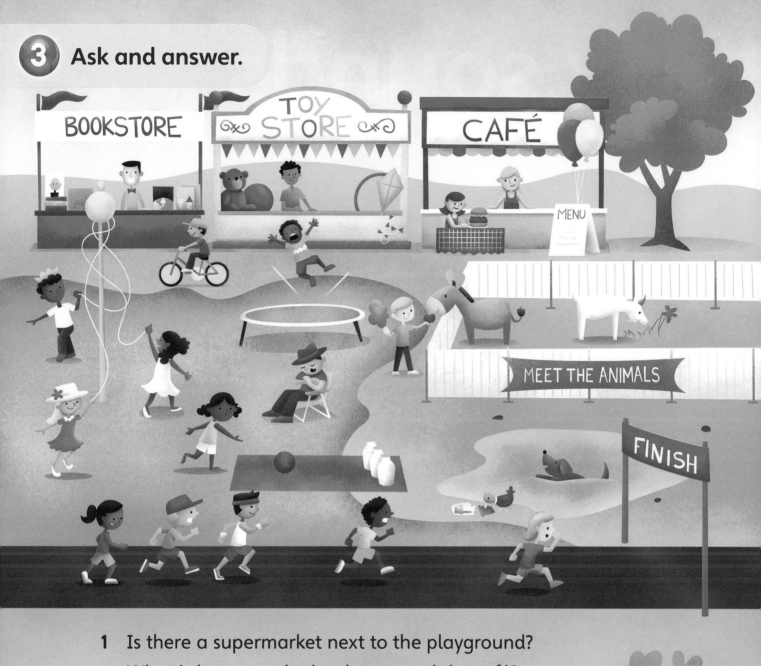

1 Is there a supermarket next to the playground?

2 What is between the bookstore and the café?

3 Is there a pond at the park?

4 What is the duck doing?

5 Is the dog sleeping?

6 What is the donkey doing?

7 Is she eating cereal?

8 What's he doing?

9 Is she swimming?

10 What's he doing?

My sounds

seal • zebra

camel • kangaroo

queen bee • ox

wolf • whale

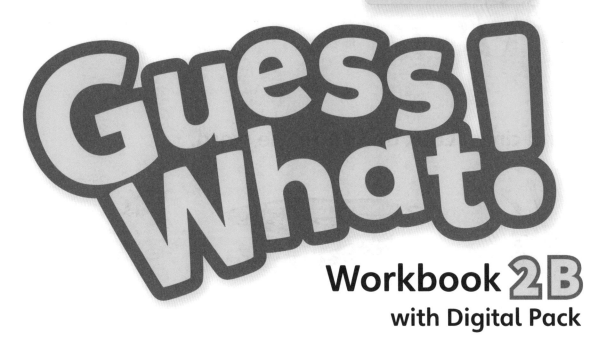

UPDATED EDITION

Guess What!

Workbook 2B

with Digital Pack

Contents

American English

Susan Rivers

Series Editor: Lesley Koustaff

 CAMBRIDGE

1 **Find and circle. Look and write the word.**

1

rice

2

3

4

5

6

peascarrotscereal(rice)toastfish

2 **Look, read, and write yes or no.**

1 There's meat on the table.
yes

2 There are peas on the table.

3 There are potatoes on the table. _____

4 There are sausages on the table. _____

5 There's cereal on the table.

3 🎧 5.05 📄 **Listen and stick.**

1

2

3

4

5

4 (Think) **Look and write the words.**

| ~~toast~~ | cereal | peas | rice | meat |
| fish | sausages | potatoes | carrots |

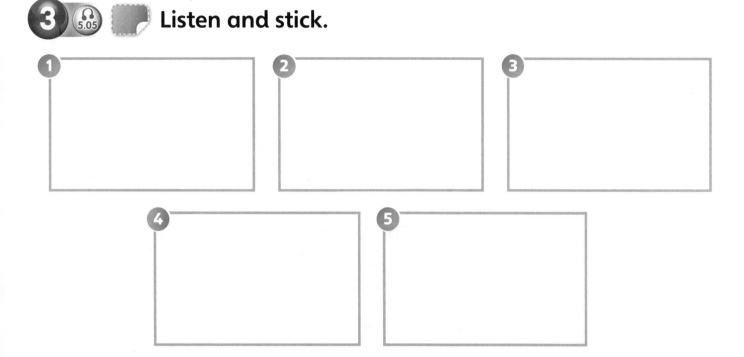

These foods are plants.	These foods aren't plants.
toast	

My picture dictionary Go to page 84: Check the words you know and trace.

5 🎧 5.08 **Listen and match. Draw a happy face or a sad face.**

6 **Look, read, and circle the words.**

1

She **likes** / **doesn't like** fish.

2

He **likes** / **doesn't like** cereal.

3

She **likes** / **doesn't like** meat.

4

He **likes** / **doesn't like** peas.

7 **Look, read, and circle the words. Then answer the questions.**

Kim

Jim

1 Does Kim like (cereal) / **sausages**?
Yes, she does.

2 Does Kim like **toast** / **peas**?
No, she doesn't.

3 Does Kim like toast, for breakfast?
Yes, she does.

4 Does Kim like sausages?
_____

1 Does Jim like **carrots** / **potatoes**?
Yes, he does.

2 Does Jim like **steak** / **fish**?
No, he doesn't.

3 Does Jim like steak, for lunch?
_____

4 Does Jim like potatoes?
_____

8 (About Me) **Draw and say. Then write and circle.**

My mom likes meat and carrots for dinner. She doesn't like fish.

My _____ likes _____ and _____ for dinner. He / She doesn't like _____ .

Look and write the words. Then listen and check.

likes   fish   please   ~~lunch~~   peas   Cake

1

Look! Café Hawaii!

Café Hawaii

Let's go for _lunch_ !

2

Café Hawaii

Would you like _____ and potatoes?

Yes, please!   No, thank you!

3

What about carrots or _____ , iPal?

No, thank you!

4

Oh, dear! What would you like, iPal?

_____ ! I like chocolate cake.

5

More cake, _____ !

No, iPal. That's enough!

6

What's the matter?

He _____ chocolate cake – a lot!

10 **Look, read, and stick.**

I eat healthy food.

11 **Trace the letters.**

A seal in the sun. A zebra in the zoo.

12  **Listen and circle _s_ or _z_.**

1

(S) Z

2

S Z

3

S Z

4

S Z

What kind of **food** is it?

1 Look and write the words in the chart.

peas

sausages

rice

carrots

fish

cheese

milk

bread

fruits and vegetables	meat and fish	grains and cereals	dairy
peas			

Evaluation

1 **Read and write the word.**

1 T o a s t is bread.
2 C _ _ _ _ _ _ _ are orange. They come from plants.
3 F _ _ _ live in water. They can swim.
4 P _ _ _ are very small and green. They come from plants.
5 Chicken and sausages are m _ _ _ .
6 R _ _ _ is small and white. It comes from plants.

2 **What's your favorite part? Use your stickers.**

story   song   video

3 **Puzzle** **What's different? Circle and write.**
Then go to page 88 and write the letters.

___ ___ ___ ___
7

6 Activities

1 **Look, match, and write.**

1  2  3  4

a   b    c    d

ride a _____   play _____   fly a _____   take *photographs*

2 **Look and write the words.**

| ~~play~~ take ride fly play roller-skate |

1

A: Let's play tennis. Can you __play__ tennis?

B: No, I can't, but I can _____ basketball.

2

A: Can you _____ a horse?

B: Yes, I can, and I can _____ a kite, too.

3

A: I can roller-skate. Can you _____ ?

B: No, I can't, but I can _____ photographs!

3   **Listen and stick.**

4 **Look and write the words.**

ride a horse ~~play basketball~~ play tennis
roller-skate take photographs play baseball

play basketball

My picture dictionary → **Go to page 85: Check the words you know and trace.**

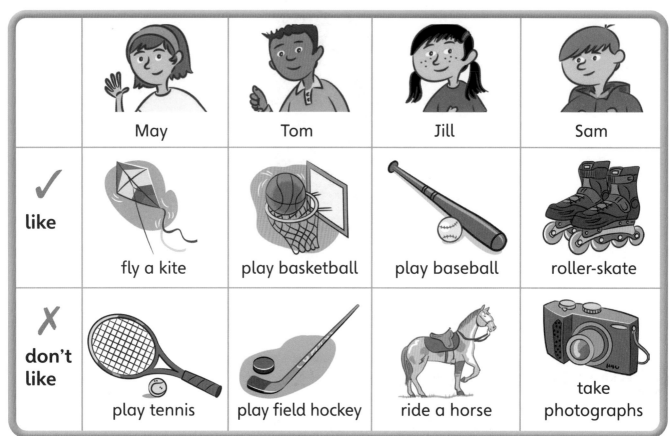

	May	Tom	Jill	Sam
✓ **like**	fly a kite	play basketball	play baseball	roller-skate
✗ **don't like**	play tennis	play field hockey	ride a horse	take photographs

1  I **like** / **don't like** playing tennis.

2  I **like** / **don't like** playing field hockey.

3  I **like** / **don't like** riding a horse.

4  I **like** / **don't like** taking photographs.

5 May ___*likes*___ flying a kite.

6 Tom _____ playing basketball.

7 Jill _____ playing baseball.

8 Sam _____ roller-skating.

6 Look, read, and circle the answers.

1

Do you like taking photographs?

(Yes, I do.) / No, I don't.

2

Do you like playing tennis?

Yes, I do. / No, I don't.

3

Does he like playing baseball?
Yes, he does. / No, he doesn't.

4

Does she like flying a kite?
Yes, she does. / No, she doesn't.

7 (About Me) Complete the chart. Ask and answer.

Do you like riding a horse?

Yes, I do.

No, I don't.

Do you like ...	riding a horse?	_____ ?	_____ ?
1 Me	yes / no	yes / no	yes / no
2 _____	yes / no	yes / no	yes / no
3 _____	yes / no	yes / no	yes / no

I like ...

_____ likes ...

8 🎧 6.11 **Read and number. Then listen and check.**

a
HOME GUEST
Good job, Olivia!
Thanks, iPal.

b
I'm sorry.
That's OK.

c
The *All Stars* are my favorite team!
Let's play! Put on these shirts!

d
HOME GUEST
Watch me! Throw the ball like this.
Yes!

e
HOME GUEST
That's not fair!
Play nicely, iPal.

f
It's a basketball!
Are you OK, David?

1

9   **Look, unscramble, and stick.**

a

b

I (lypa) _____ nicely.

10 **Trace the letters.**

A camel with a camera. A kangaroo with a kite.

11 (6.14) **Listen and number the pictures.**

a 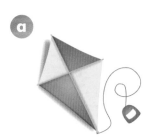 ☐

b  ☐

c  ☐

d  ☐

e  1

f  ☐

What **equipment** do we need?

1 **Look and match the pictures.**

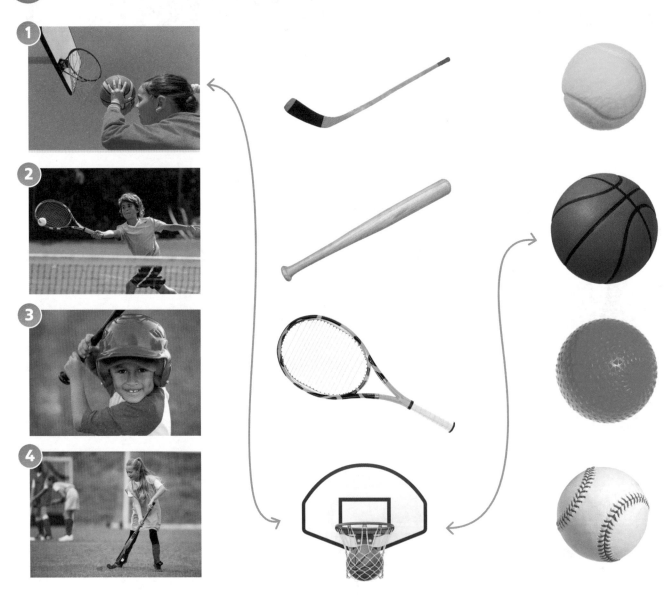

2 **Look at Activity 1 and write the words.**

1 I play basketball with a ___basket___ and a ___ball___ .
2 I play tennis with a _____ and a _____ .
3 I play baseball with a _____ and a _____ .
4 I play field hockey with a _____ and a _____ .

Evaluation

1 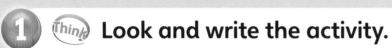 **Look and write the activity.**

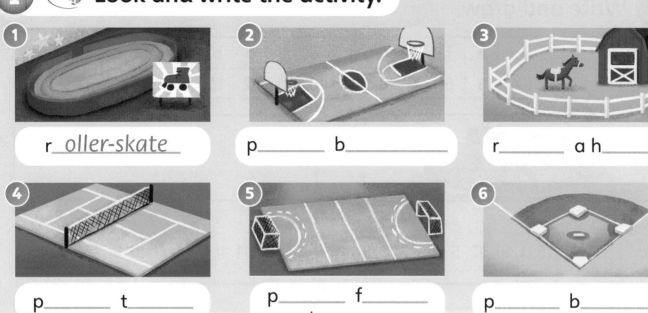

1 r _oller-skate_

2 p_____ b_____

3 r_____ a h_____

4 p_____ t_____

5 p_____ f_____ h_____

6 p_____ b_____

2 **What's your favorite part? Use your stickers.**

story   song   video

3 **Puzzle** **What's different? Circle and write. Then go to page 88 and write the letters.**

___ ___ ___ ___   ___ ___ ___ ___ ___ ___
      4   2

Review Units 5 and 6

1 Write and draw.

a	b	c	d	e	f	g	h	i	k	l	o	p	r	s	t	u	y
1	2	3	4	5	6	7	8	9	10	11	12	13	14	15	16	17	18

1

p o t a t o e s
13 12 16 1 16 12 5 15

2

_ _ _ _ _ _ _ _
6 11 18 1 10 9 16 5

3

_ _ _ _ _ _ _ _
15 1 17 15 1 7 5 15

4

_ _ _ _ _ _ _ _ _ _ _ _ _ _
13 11 1 18 2 1 15 10 5 16 2 1 11 11

5

_ _ _ _ _ _
3 5 14 5 1 11

6

_ _ _ _ _ _ - _ _ _ _ _
14 12 11 11 5 14 15 10 1 16 5

2 Read and match.

1	He likes	a	field hockey.
2	She doesn't	b	beans.
3	Does he	c	taking photographs?
4	I like playing	d	toast.
5	He doesn't like	e	like playing tennis?
6	Do you like	f	like meat.

3 **Look, read, and write the words.**

roller-skating   rice   ~~photographs~~   fish   ~~do~~   doesn't   does   don't

1

Do you like taking _photographs_ ?
Yes, I ___do___ .

2

Does she like _____ ?
Yes, she _____ .

3

Does he like _____ ?
No, he _____ .

4

Do you like _____ ?
No, I _____ .

4 🎧 6.17 **Listen and check ✓.**

1

2

In town

1 Look at the picture and write the letter.

1 street __e__	**2** café _____
3 school _____	**4** bookstore _____
5 playground _____	**6** supermarket _____

2 Look at Activity 1 and write *yes* or *no*.

1 There's a toy store in the town. __no__
2 There's a playground in the town. _____
3 There's a movie theater in the town. _____
4 There's a café in the town. _____
5 There's a clothing store in the town. _____
6 There's a school in the town. _____

3 7.05 **Listen and stick.**

1

2

3

4

5

4 (Think) **Look and write.**

1

toy store

2

3

4

My picture dictionary → Go to page 86: Check the words you know and trace.

5 Think Look, read, and match.

1 next to

2 in front of

3 behind

4 between

6 Look, read, and circle the words.

1 The school is **behind** / (**next to**) the playground.

2 The toy store is **in front of** / **between** the bookstore and the clothing store.

3 The tree is **next to** / **in front of** the movie theater.

4 The supermarket is **behind** / **between** the park.

7 About Me Draw and say. Then write.

My school is next to the park.

My school is _____
_____ .

8 **Look, read, and check ✓.**

1 Is there a toy store next to the school?

Yes, there is. ☐   No, there isn't. ✓

2 Is there a café in front of the supermarket?

Yes, there is. ☐   No, there isn't. ☐

3 Is there a toy store between the bookstore and the school?

Yes, there is. ☐   No, there isn't. ☐

4 Is there a playground behind the school?

Yes, there is. ☐   No, there isn't. ☐

9 **Complete the questions and the answers.**

1 ___Is there___ a park next to the bookstore?
No, ___there isn't___ .

2 _____ a playground between the school and the supermarket?
No, _____ .

3 _____ a street in front of the café?
Yes, _____ .

4 _____ a park behind the supermarket?
Yes, _____ .

10 🎧 7.11 Read and write the letter. Then listen and check.

a No, iPal! Be careful!

b I like going to the movies.

c Movie tickets!

d Oh, no! It's closed today!

e Look left and right.

f Where's the movie theater?

1 — C — They're from my cousin, Anna!

2 — It's next to the supermarket.

3 — Let's go!

4 — It's safe now. Let's cross.

5 — Come with me!

6 — It's a movie about robots!

11 Look, unscramble, and stick.

I am (esfa) _____ .

12 Trace the letters.

A quick queen bee. An ox with an X-ray.

13 7.14 Listen and write *qu* or *x*.

1

_qu_een bee

2

6

si__

3

o__

4

____ick

Where are the places?

1 Look, read, and circle the word.

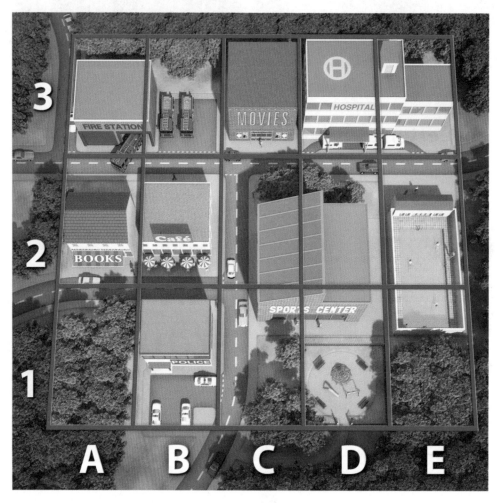

1 There's a (fire station) / police station in A3.
2 There's a movie theater / bookstore in C3.
3 There's a café / hospital in B2.
4 There's a sports center / park in D1.

2 Look at Activity 1 and answer the questions.

1 Where's the police station? _____B1_____
2 Where's the bookstore? _____
3 Where's the hospital? _____
4 Where's the sports center? _____

Evaluation

1 (Think) **Look and write the word.**

1

supermarket

2
_____

3
_____

4
_____

5
_____

6
_____

2 **What's your favorite part? Use your stickers.**

story	song	video
◯	◯	◯

3 (Puzzle) **What's different? Circle and write.**
Then go to page 88 and write the letters.

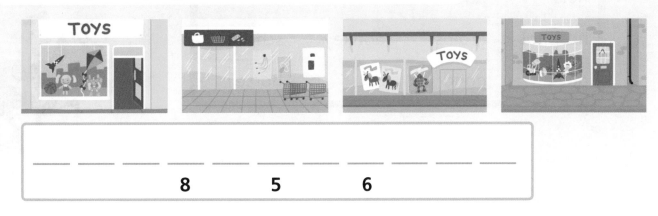

TOYS   TOYS   TOYS

_____ _____ _____ _____ _____ _____ _____ _____ _____
        8   5   6

8 On the farm

1 Look, read, and circle the word.

1 (cow) / horse

2 sheep / goat

3 barn / field

4 horse / donkey

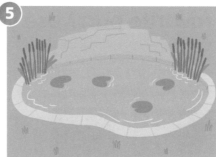

5 field / pond

6 duck / donkey

2 Follow the animal words.

Start →

cow	goat	park	barn
field	duck	sheep	air
hospital	grains	donkey	school
dairy	pond	cat	horse

Good job!

3 🎧 8.05 📄 Listen and stick.

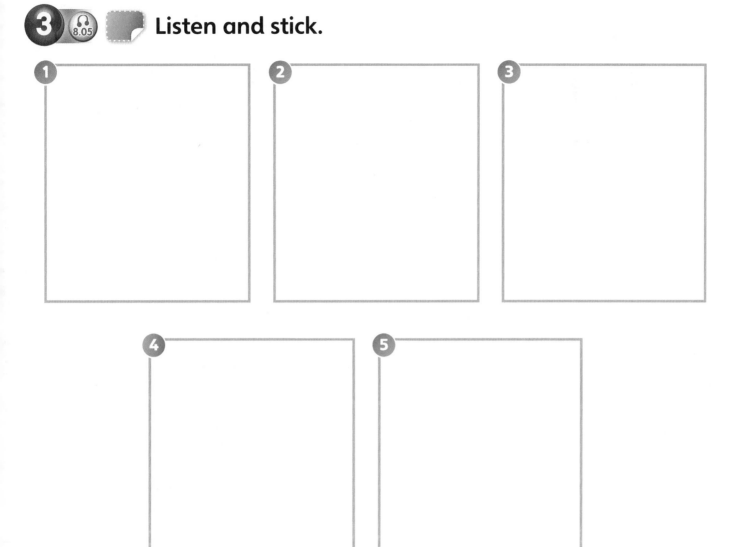

1
2
3
4
5

4 Think Read and write the word.

1 Milk comes from this animal. It isn't a goat. _____COW_____

2 This animal can swim and fly. It likes water. _____

3 We can ride this animal. It's not a donkey. _____

4 Wool comes from this animal. _____

5 This is a house for cows and horses. _____

6 Fish and ducks swim in this. _____

My picture dictionary Go to page 87: Check the words you know and trace.

5 Look, read, and check ✓.

1

The cow is eating. ✓

The cow is jumping. ☐

2

The horse is running. ☐

The horse is sleeping. ☐

3

The duck is flying. ☐

The duck is swimming. ☐

6 Look, read, and answer the questions.

1

What's the donkey doing?

It's eating.

2

What's the duck doing?

_____

3

What's the goat doing?

_____

4

What's the sheep doing?

_____

7 (About Me) Draw your favorite farm animal. Then write.

This is a _____ .

It's _____ .

8 **Listen and check ✓ or put an ✗.**

1
 ✓

2
 ☐

3
 ☐

4
 ☐

9 **Look, read, and circle the word.**

1

Is the horse **eating /(sleeping)**?
No, it isn't.

2

Is the cow **running / sleeping**?
Yes, it is.

3

Is the goat **sleeping / jumping**?
No, it isn't.

4

Is the duck **swimming / flying**?
Yes, it is.

5

Is the sheep **eating / running**?
No, it isn't.

6

Is the horse **sleeping / swimming**?
No, it isn't.

10 🎧 8.11 Look and write the words. Then listen and check.

party   ~~iPal~~   dancing   Goodbye   flying   Welcome

1

It's a message for _iPal_ .

Let's find him!

2

Would you like to come to a _____?

Yes, please!

3

Hold on!

We're _____!

4

_____ to the party!

It's so nice to see you!

WELCOME HOME iPAL

5

What's Ben doing?

He's ... _____!

6

_____, iPal!

Goodbye! Thanks for taking care of me!

11 Look, unscramble, and stick.

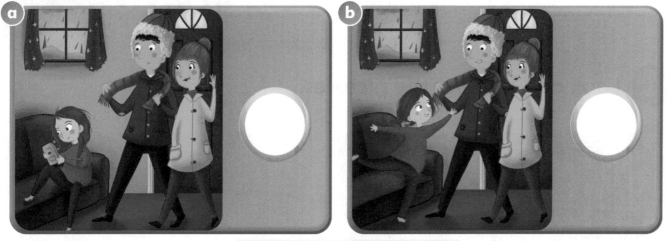

a

b

I love my (ehmo) _____ .

12 Trace the letters.

A wolf in the water.
A white whale with
a wheel.

13 8.14 Listen and put a check ✓ next to *w* or *wh*.

1	w ✓	wh ☐	2	w ☐	wh ☐
3	w ☐	wh ☐	4	w ☐	wh ☐

What do farmers do?

1 Look and number the pictures.

a

b

c

d

1

2 Look at Activity 1 and write the letter.

1 A farmer turns soil. `b`

2 A farmer plants seeds.

3 A farmer waters plants.

4 A farmer harvests plants.

Evaluation

1 **Write the words and find.**

1. COW
2. _____
3. _____
4. _____
5. _____
6. _____

```
s h e e p a c n (c o w) o
g a d o n k e y m k l p
c b a r n o l p a t u e
f i e l d g h n a o q i
a f p o n d g r t e y a
```

2 **What's your favorite part? Use your stickers.**

story   song   video

3 **Puzzle** **What's different? Circle and write.
Then go to page 88 and write the letters.**

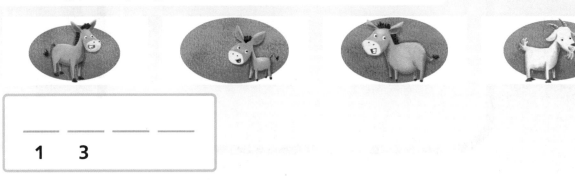

____ ____ ____ ____
1   3

81

Review Units 7 and 8

1 Look and write the word. Then draw Number 11.

1 | s | u | p | e | r | m | a | r | k | e | t |

82

2 Look, read, and write the answers.

1

What's the goat doing?

It's jumping.

2

Is there a park next to the supermarket?

_____

3

Is the sheep running?

_____

4

What's the horse doing?

_____

3 Listen and check ✓.

1

2

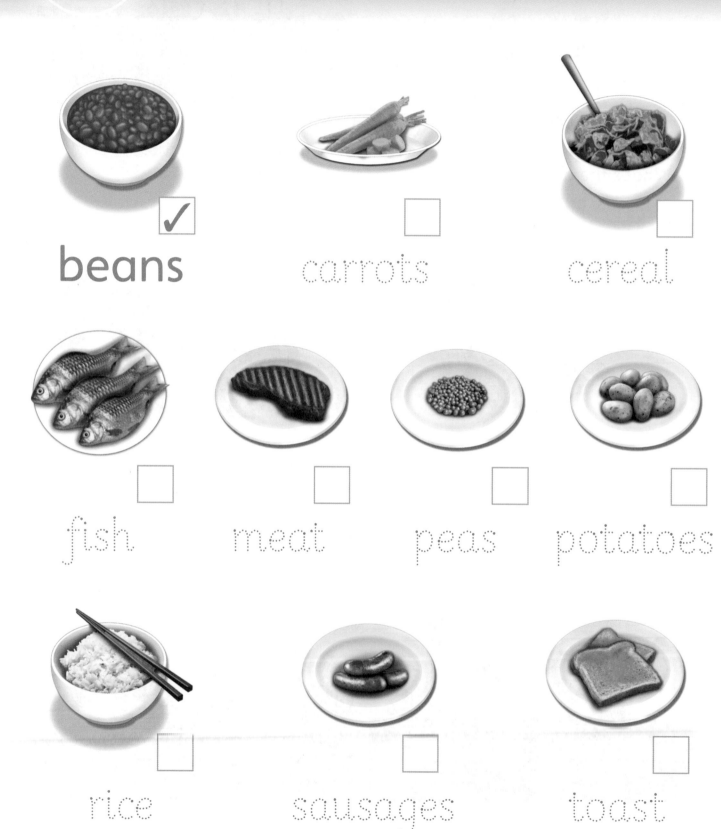

beans ✓

carrots ☐

cereal ☐

fish ☐

meat ☐

peas ☐

potatoes ☐

rice ☐

sausages ☐

toast ☐

6 Activities

 ✓

fly a kite

 ☐

play baseball

 ☐

play basketball

 ☐

play field hockey

 ☐

take photographs

 ☐

ride a horse

 ☐

roller-skate

 ☐

play tennis

7 In town

bookstore ✓

café

movie theater

clothing store

park

play- ground

school

street

supermarket

toy store

8 On the farm

 ✓

barn

cow

donkey

duck

field

goat

horse

pond

sheep

My puzzle

1 Write the letters in the correct place.

```
_ _ _ _    J O B,    _ Y    F _ _ _ N D !
1 2 3 4              5      6 7 8
```

Acknowledgments

Many thanks to everyone in the excellent team at Cambridge University Press & Assessment in Spain, the UK, and India.

The authors and publishers would like to thank the following contributors:

Blooberry Design: concept design, cover design, book design
Hyphen: publishing management, page make-up
Ann Thomson: art direction
Gareth Boden: commissioned photography
Jon Barlow: commissioned photography
Ian Harker: class audio recording
John Marshall Media: "Grammar fun" recordings
Robert Lee, Dib Dib Dub Studios: song and chant composition
Vince Cross: theme tune composition
James Richardson: arrangement of theme tune
Phaebus: "CLIL" video production
Kiki Foster: "Look!" video production
Bill Smith Group: "Grammar fun" and story animations
Sounds Like Mike Ltd: "Grammar Fun" video production

The authors and publishers acknowledge the following sources of copyright material and are grateful for the permissions granted. While every effort has been made, it has not always been possible to identify the sources of all the material used, or to trace all copyright holders. If any omissions are brought to our notice, we will be happy to include the appropriate acknowledgements on reprinting and in the next update to the digital edition, as applicable.

Key: U = Unit.

Student's Book

Photography

The following photos are sourced from Getty Images:

U5: Andrew Olney/Stockbyte; Adam Gault/OJO Images ; bluehill75/E+; Mohd Haniff Abas/EyeEm; Stockbyte; FatCamera/E+; John A. Rizzo/Photodisc; Juanmonino/E+; AdShooter/E+; Mohd Haniff Abas /EyeEm; Stockbyte/Stockbyte; **U6:** Leander Baerenz/Getty Images ; Hybrid Images/Getty Images; Lauri Patterson/Getty Images; Image Source; Glyn Jones/Corbis/VCG; Yevgen Romanenko/Moment; Lawrence Manning/Corbis; Blake Little/Stone; George Doyle/Stockbyte; Photodisc; **U7:** lucentius/iStock/Getty Images Plus; Andersen Ross Photography Inc/DigitalVision/Getty images; AlexSava/E+; Marje/E+; Poh Kim Yeoh/EyeEm; MirageC/Moment; David Zaitz/The Image Bank Unreleased; Andersen Ross Photography Inc/DigitalVision; 500px Asia; LordRunar/E+; Nipitphon Na Chiangmai/EyeEm; Nipitphon Na Chiangmai/EyeEm; **U8:** BlazenImages/iStock/Getty Images Plus; Stephen Dorey/Getty Images; SCIENCE PHOTO LIBRARY; kickstand/E+; Burazin/The Image Bank; Life On White/Photodisc; Supawat Punnanon/EyeEm; Igor Alecsander/E+; Theerasak Tammachuen/EyeEm; Floortje/E+; Image Source.

The following photos are sourced from other libraries:

U5: Naho Yoshizawa/Shutterstock; Craig Richardson/Alamy; Tracy Whiteside/Alamy; Tetra Images,LLC/Alamy; Tracy Whiteside/Alamy; Stefano Politi Markovina/Alamy Stock Photo; matka_Wariatka/Shutterstock; Kolpakova Svetlana/Shutterstock; Jag_cz/Shutterstock; Christine Langer-Pueschel/Shutterstock; Christian Draghici/Shutterstock; koss13/Shutterstock; Christian Jung/Shutterstock; Africa Studio/Shutterstock; **U6:** Dan Thornberg/Shutterstock; Krakenimages.com/Shutterstock; Hurst Photo/Shutterstock; Alex White/Shutterstock; taelove7/Shutterstock; J.Helgason/Shutterstock; gorillaimages/Shutterstock; Veronica Louro/Shutterstock; Ramona Heim/Shutterstock; Rob Bouwman/Shutterstock; J. Helgason/Shutterstock; Production Perig/Shutterstock; Production Perig/Shutterstock; Phovoir/Shutterstock; ESB Professional/Shutterstock; Kuttig - People/Alamy; F1online digitale Bildagentur GmbH/Alamy; David Madison/DigitalVision; pukach/Shutterstock; anaken2012/Shutterstock; Image Source Plus/Alamy; Thyrymn2/Alamy; onilmilk/Shutterstock; Sean Gladwell/Shutterstock; Aaron Amat/Shutterstock; mexrix/Shutterstock; Pal2iyawit/Shutterstock; Ledo/Shutterstock; Nattika/Shuterstock; Ramon grosso dolarea/Shutterstock; Lotus_studio/Shutterstock; Bits And Splits/Shutterstock; Joe Gough/Shutterstock; Elnur/Shutterstock; Tracy Whiteside/Shutterstock; oliveromg/Shutterstock; Igor Dutina/Shutterstock; StockPhotosArt/Shutterstock; Leonid Shcheglov/Shutterstock.; **U7:** Gladskikh Tatiana/Shutterstock; Pavel L Photo and Video/Shutterstock; stockfour/Shutterstock; Carlos Yudica/Shutterstock; Brett Baunton/Alamy; A.P.S.(UK)/Alamy; meunierd/Shutterstock; Mike Robinson/Alamy; **U8:** Dieter Hawlan/Shutterstock; Orhan Cam/Shutterstock; Sebastian Knight/Shutterstock; Luca Santilli/Shutterstock; Joseph Sohm/Shutterstock; Scott Prokop/Shutterstock; BrianGoodman/Shutterstock; Diane Picard/Shutterstock; Schubbel/Shutterstock; Ewa Studio/Shutterstock; Makarova Viktoria/Shutterstock; Kemeo/Shutterstock; val lawless/Shutterstock; Alexander Matvienko/Alamy; Jolanta Wojcicka/Shutterstock; Danylo Saniylenko/Shutterstock; Tim Scrivener/Alamy; Keith Dannemiller/Corbis; Alex Treadway/National Geographic Society/Corbis; Tim Scrivener/Alamy Stock Photo; Arterra Picture Library/Alamy; THP Creative/Shutterstock; Brandon Seidel/Shutterstock; 1stGallery/Shutterstock; Denise Lett/Shutterstock; imageBROKER/Alamy; IxMaster/Shutterstock; Tetra Images/Alamy Stock Photo; Alinute Silzeviciute/Shutterstock; imageBROKER.com GmbH & Co. KG/Alamy Stock Photo.

Workbook

Photography

The following photos are sourced from Getty Images:

U5: Food style and photography/Moment; DebbiSmirnoff/E+; **U6:** SerrNovik/iStock/Getty Images Plus; David Madison/DigitalVision; Stockbyte; C-You/iStock/Getty Images Plus; **U7:** lucentius/iStock/Getty Images Plus; **U8:** BlazenImages/iStock/Getty Images Plus; Stephen Dorey/Stockbyte Unreleased; xalanx/iStock/Getty Images Plus; fotokostic/iStock/Getty Images Plus; Echo/Cultura/Getty Images.

The following photos are sourced from other libraries:

U5: Naho Yoshizawa/Corbis; Stefano Politi Markovina/Alamy; stevemart/Shutterstock; foodfolio/Alamy; kazoka/Shutterstock; Olga Miltsova/Shutterstock; Olga Nayashkova/Shutterstock; sevenke/Shutterstock; **U6:** zefart/Shutterstock; Juergen Hasenkopf/Alamy; Digital Media Pro/Shutterstock; redsnapper/Alamy; irin-k/Shutterstock; Lightspring/Shutterstock; peterboxy/Shutterstock; Dan Thornberg/Shutterstock; Vitawin/Shutterstock; mipan/Shutterstock; **U7:** A.P.S. (UK)/Alamy; **U8:** Maskot/Corbis.

Front Cover Photo by Arthur Morris/Corbis Documentary.

Illustrations

Aphik, Andy Parker; Bill Bolton; Chris Jevons (Bright Agency); Joelle Dreidemy (Bright Agency); Gareth Conway; Kirsten Collier (Bright Agency); Marcus Cutler (Sylvie Poggio); Marek Jagucki; Phil Garner (Beehive Illustration); Richard Watson (Bright Agency); Woody Fox (Bright Agency); Barbara Bakos (Bright Agency); Humberto Blanco (Sylvie Poggio Agency); Kimberley Barnes (Bright Agency); Lucy Fleming (Bright Agency); Monkey Feet.

Unit 5

Unit 6

Evaluation

Values